Enough is Enough by AL Poole

To my loving, supportive and strong Adults

Asia Marshalle Poole
&
Kortney Alexander Poole

For I tried to be the Best Mother I could. But life happens and We Stand.........

"With God's help all things are POSSIBLE"

Chapter 1   (The beginning of the End)

Lee started telling me about a dream he had the night before. I really wasn't interested nor in the mood to hear what he had to say. I was leaving for good this time!

It's funny how God gives you clues for life. It's whether or not we choose to revive them.

Lee's dream was he had seen his sister and mother. They kept telling him to let me go. It felt like he just couldn't. He walked around the apartment following me. As I checked for everything of ours I had packed. You see it was 4am the movers were scheduled for 8am. Lee angrily said, "Alexandria you will not leave me!" I looked unsurprised . His breathing changed as a bear that confirmed his dinner beating his chest. His eyes had a sorrowful look of longing. His sex had risen for just these occassuon. This was a usual tack tick for Lee. Sex flowers I'm sorry then full bloom rage that cound'nt be restrained. I slowly moved as tho he had me in a trans. Lee reached out for me and said "I'm horny" I quickly responded with "I'm sure you are, there's nothing I can do about that or for you! I snapped back into reality and swiftly moved out of the bathroom.

I think how much time I've wasted trying to love a man that never felt or even understood the meaning of the word.

You see Lee was a man with a hardened heart. From his mother, siblings, wife, son and now me. We met while my small children waved for a Park Concert to start. I had brought my picnic basket so we could hear while we listened to the music.

Suddenly a tall dark man with a Kangol hat approached us. "Are you waiting for someone? He asked, with a chest cat grin. Sun glaring into my eyes, "Yes we are waiting for the concert to start. Oh! You are a week early , he grinned. I sat there in pure embarrassment for a moment. I'll go get you a schedule and then you'll know for sure the days. As I watched this man of substance and knowledge. I got hot!! I had forgotten how long it had been since I had been with a man. Quickly I snapped out that thought, then started to gather our things from the picnic and children in tow. As we reached the car, he came back with a brochure. I thanked him as I was packing my car.. "Hopefully I'll see you next week. He briskly walked off. We got into the car and never looked back.

CHAPTER 2

The kids' dad and I have been together for three years. Their dad had gone out to get pampers and never came back. It sounds funny but true. We started our day with daycare, work, church and home. We moved to a small town in Utah. It would be the last place our family would find us.

One morning going through the routine. I was on my way to work sitting down at my desk. The phone rang. It was the daycare, telling me Ericka had been in an accident. I hadn't even hung up the phone when I ran out of my office to my car. As I arrived the teachers braced me for the worst.

They told me she was sitting at a picnic table, 8bent over to look at her shoe and fell. She had a bloody nose a black eye. It looked like someone beat my child. We immediately went to the Dr. I knew she didn't just fall. Ericka was 3 years old, light skinned and very shy. She barely spoke to anyone but me and her brother.   It's so hard to imagine someone touched a child in this way. I knew that this person knew the difference from a woman to a child. But back in those days we could try our own kind or so I thought. Needless to say, I went to the police. Someone was going to pay! When I arrived, I asked to speak to the investigation officer. The policeman with strong browneyes directed me into a room with a table and two chairs. Just like in the movies. I sat there in that room for about 30 mins. As I wondered what was taking so long a short oversized man burst in the door. He slammed his briefcase on the table. He took a seat without saying a word. I got angrier. No one seems to take me seriously. But why would they? This was unheard of! As I started to explain what happened to my daughter the detective was pulling out paper. It was quite obvious he knew; the daycare knew. They had tipped the police before I got there. At the end of our conversation the detective told me one thing. "You watch too much TV". Because I asked for a line up? I may have been guilty of that, but I saw through everyone involved I was certain that one day the truth would come out. You see it wasn't my battle. Sometimes we mean I. Certainly, none of you would not fight for your child! Especially When you have done all you can to protect, provide and pray since the day you were conceived.   I trusted God then and now I trust God with my Life! As years went by and life started to become normal (whatever that is) I went over how I let this happen. I never figured that out. Some things we just don't need to know.

Chapter 3

(The children and Me)

Ericka stayed at home with me. I couldn't sleep or eat. All I did was walk aimlessly in circles. No one knew my deepest past.

While in the Navy I was almost raped by my roommate and his friends. By the grace of GOD my other roommate came home dying early to get lunch and so paperwork. When I think back, I would have taken it had I known it would happen to my daughter years later.   I often sit and think why would God let that happen to a child? I may never know.

Ericka and I sat all day studying ABC and looked for another daycare. I was in no shape, but I had to work. We found a better daycare and closer to home. Mrs. Haynes Daycare. Funny I really can't remember you both being there. But I know you do. When we would talk about the ole days you enjoyed over there. My work and trying to stay ahead. Please don't think I was abandoned by children. Because I didn't. Everywhere you saw my children you saw me. I have a son who is only a few years apart. Eric is his name. Eric stayed in his books. He didn't talk much only when necessary. Being a single parent in the 90's was an easy thing to do. Almost always my children and I had to eat made up dishes. Made up by whatever I had in the cabinet and refrigerator to get creative. When things were tight, we would eat cereal for dinner. Eric and Ericka were delighted when we had pancakes! It was a meal as far as I was concerned. Even with 3 jobs it was tight. Any single mom can tell you it's a JOB!

Life went on for us.! We found another church and God was never lost! We stayed with my mother when we moved back to Salt Lake, Utah. It was a quiet little town.

This is where I had my children and what I thought was the perfect little family. Eric played soccer and Ericka was very shy and quiet. I tried to keep them involved with outside activities to get them well rounded. I found The Boys and Girls club at the YMCA. The children made new friends and led a normal life or so I thought.

As days become weeks and weeks become months Eric became more involved with his friends. He was a loner.
He was very smart. Things seem to come naturally for him. He was always getting an award for something at school. I was very proud of him. Ericka started to come around and hang with her new friends. I was pleased she came out of the shell. It was almost as though something was wrong, but I could not figure it out. So, I let her grow. Like the word says, "your children and children's children shall be blessed beyond measure." I know they were.
blessed I could see it in both their eyes. This is a Love that is close to GOD. I have prayed over them all their lives.

One day my children came home to tell me they almost got hit walking across a busy street. This was their usual path to school. But there was something different. We did our morning routine. Our prayer of 1 Chronicles 4:10. I felt relieved and very calm. Erika shouted, "Mom you should have seen it! It floated out of nowhere and stood in front of the bus. Eric, chimed in. "It was an Angel! She stood between us and the Bus! As I stood there listening to both of their matter-of-fact stories. Their faces glowed that they had been anointed and Blessed by God. From that day forward I knew that God took and will always be there for us!

Erika became quite a handful as she got older. She was very rebellious and disrespectful to herself, others and me. I did everything I could to keep her on the straight and narrow.

Chapter 4

Salt as we called it was a small town in Utah. Everyone new everyone. Life was slow and safe. My family only seemed close when death would strike us. We all lived close to one another not more than a few blocks apart.

I found a job at the local hospital called "Salt". Everything was good! I know there is a GOD. You see, I had many conversations with him. Everything came true. I had two smart and beautiful children, a beautiful home. I lacked the love of my life. I banned myself from work, church and home for 3 straight years.

After the incident with Lee, I was bound to find help for me and my children. Mentally these things happened. But I never thought of it happening to us. Were there signs that I had missed? Did I want to bury it like everything else? No, I couldn't give up! It was burning inside of me, and I was beyond curious. As I dropped the kids at the Boys/Girls club I saw a flier on the bulletin board, "Domestic Violence" Have you been hurt and stuck and nowhere to turn? It was a blue flier at the bottom it read YWCA Women's group. Just what I needed. Now more than ever. On Thursday was the next meeting. I walked in afraid I might see someone I knew; you see being in a middle-class, single mother and black I never thought it could happen to me. But there I was trying to find me. She got lost being married to Lee eleven years. I often thought how different things could be if I hadn't married him.   I was so desperate. Yes, I am the one who got it all. Two years of Yeah see I am married now. No one cared and as it was kept, everyone was laughing at me anyway. The next 9 years were hell. I kept going to the YWCA meetings and my mind got stronger. I prayed every day. I would wake up and pray (a friend's grandmother told me that when "God has your undivided attention, and you must heed) My mind would race while I tried to make things better for me and my children. One day while driving around town I came across a school that had just opened. So, I decided to check it out. It was worth a try. The school was brand new and offered a lot of programs. I talked with a counselor, Mr. Pitt. He was very knowledgeable of all the programs for my schedule to attend. He asked me questions of where I wanted to be in 5 years? What I wanted to do. As I sat there and listened to the questions my mind wandered into a high rise office with a city view of downtown. A lawyer! That's it! I wanted to change laws of domestic violence. Since I had firsthand experience and the classes at the YWCA I could do it. With GOD's there was nothing I wouldn't do!

 So I enrolled in June in 1998. My life was going somewhere. I signed up for a Paralegal program. This is a dream come true. Deep down inside I knew I could do it if I put my mind to it. When I got home that evening, I found the kids playing video games. Erika was 10 and Eric was 12. I sat them both down and explained I was going to school too! Not just school but college. I embedded myself in them to get an education or learn a trade. But do what you enjoy!   Life can be whatever you want. If you can think about it, you can see it. If it's in your heart, make it come out of your mouth and speak it as though it were!

I know you can be sure that "Angel" my children saw would be around a long time!

Those will be faces that I'll never forget. All children should be an inspiration to us adults.

As my classes started, I was so excited. I promised myself to stay focused. No outside activities (partying, hanging out another job not even dating was out.) I Loved the law. The changes in history. The test seems to come naturally. I believed I was at the right place at the right time. While I dug deep into my studies my children started growing up. Eric was driving and Erika was into boys and not just a tomboy. So, I decided after school I'd go into the military. Now that I think of it, I should have gone into the military then school. I graduated 2nd in my class 6 mos. Early. My new friend Becky. We were the eldest in class and took it very seriously. Becky was 1st and you be sure I stayed glued to her. She was from Iowa. Becky had blonde hair and blue eyes. She reminded me of an older Marilyn Monroe. Becky could drink like a fish, and I kept up with her with that too. She was truly a cool friend.

After graduation I gave myself a going away party. I was proud of myself. I was the first born to graduate from college in my immediate family. My parents had me and at that time they couldn't do anything but work.

I would do everything I could to make them proud of me. Nothing seems to phase them. So, I became, as my mother called

it "A Gypsy". I was one before I had children. I would work, travel.
and be me.   I talked to my mom and brother. They agreed to watch my teens as I went into the military for the second time. I decided the Navy was the best for me. As I packed up my things, I wonder what GOD had for me. I wanted to see the world and so I did. On January 2nd I shipped out to Orlando, Fla! Back then you could sign up and months later you could be sent to boot camp. I was so excited about my adventure, As I kissed my children, I knew that it was for the US to be better and do better. And so, it began.

Chapter 5

As I reached the gate to catch my flight there were a lot of others like me that were going to the same place. We were young but wanted change. It was 5am when we took off. The flight was full. As I got settled in my seat I decided to go to sleep. Hours later we landed in FLA. It was hot, dark and full of people in Uniform waiting for us to get off the bus. We were herded like cattle. As I took a seat a lady no more than 20 sat next to me. Her name was Kim Patters. She introduced herself and told me she was from N.C. and like me had teenagers and wanted change. We became best friends for at least 8 weeks. We finally reached the Base. As we all got off the bus a very tall white officer stood at the doorway of the bus yelling," Get off the Bus you're not with your mom Now!"

As Kim and I got off the bus we stayed close to each other from comfort. The Officer name was Wilson. She was from CA. We were told to line up in 2 rows. Instantly I realized, I AM in the Navy Now. Petty Officer 1st Class Wilson came to each one of us asking our name. It was nowhere to run, and you couldn't quit. So, we all stood there waiting for orders. We were assigned Barracks and given linen and towels. Luckily Kin and I were assigned to the same barracks. We all marched awkwardly to our respective Barracks. When we marched our way into a large room where it was nothing but metal bunk beds. Two rows each by the wall. They weren't playing when they said Boot Camp! It hit me; you signed up for this remember? So, I watched and listened. Indeed, I listened for two weeks.

By the end of the two weeks, I had everyone else got the hang of things. It basically follows the leader who played the same game. I signed up for 4 years, I liked it so much I signed up for 2 extra years. The Freedom! I felt like I could do anything. That was my problem. I didn't know what I wanted to do. BUT GOD! He had a plan for me that I just am going to try for me that I just am going to try to explain thru me to you.

Chapter 6

What can you do?

My job in the Navy was to learn how to have discipline, courage, empathy, and belief. I worked hard and played the same. Then one day this man came into my office with this strength and thug life that I liked walked into my office. I sat at my desk feeling frozen. Next thing I knew he was in my face saying my name! I felt and saw it, or so I thought. What GOD sees in a second makes us feel like a lifetime. Years went by and it was me and my little family. I came home on leave for special occasions. Family reunions, Thanksgiving, Christmas. One

Christmas Phillip and I spent with another couple which we all lived together, in a two-bedroom apartment off the Atlantic Ocean. It was beautiful. Our back bedroom windows we could look out at the ocean. That Christmas everyone was hustling and bustling around but me. I bought him a sweater that was bulky but very classy for my man. That Christmas Phillip asked me to marry him. Of course, I said Yes! I Loved him. We went to the courthouse. We were saving for our 1st home. I shared it with my family and just mentioned I was married and very happy. Neither of them said a word. I was so hurt, but now that I'm older …. I see how it feels. As my mother used to say, Karma will show up and out on you be careful! I kept being me. I went to work, became a housewife. Heck I was living the life of Riley! I still don't know who that was. At twenty-one I had a brand-new house, car and the most giving husband in the world or so I thought.   Even though Phillip had one habit that I wouldn't change. Even I indulged after being with him. I never knew that much about a "bad boy" streetside. My mother use to say, "You're so gullible. I didn't think so! As far as I was concerned, I would get so mad! But what could I do that was Mom!

Anyway, Phillip and I had a lot of other couples we hung out it. They were from all over. We were all a family or so I thought. Phillip caught me at the tender age of 21. I had no idea what I was in store for. It's funny how life can make you feel you have everything . to be young and naive I was. I had no street sense. I took those I care about the most and held on tight. I was the baby of the bunch. I loved Phillip and all I ever knew was him. Talk about rose colored glasses??? I had them. What can ti cine you do when you love someone so hard and more than you Love yourself?

Being the Believer   Chapter 8

While I lived with Phillip a couple of years he had changed. I can't really explain how or when it happened. But it did. I started going to church. If nothing else but to get some peace. The more I went the further we grew apart. Money started to come up missing. I'm not the greatest in math, but I knew when, where and how much I had. One night I fell asleep on the couch with my purse on the floor. I had checks to pay the mortgage and some cash. Can you believe the next day it was all gone! I questioned Phillip. He argued with me that he didn't take it. But who else? That night I cried out to the only one that would and could help me. JESUS, I called him out to fix this. That night I decided to go for a drive. I hit the highway driving 65 miles an hour. I had been on U6 for about 5 mins when a white thunderbird started swerving. I looked again and he started heading straight towards me! Talk about a test. I closed my eyes and my hands on the wheel. I called out his name JESUS! It was like I went into a trans. I had no control. When I opened my eyes, I was parked on the ER side of U6. The white T-bird had hit 6 other cars and on his way to the other side of the highway. I couldn't even believe what my eyes saw. I rushed home to tell Phillip and crying thanking GOD all the way. Phillip was in bed waiting on me. I told him what happened. That's when he broke down and asked for help. You can be sure Phillip and I both were being believers. We saw each other in a gently, loving and kind space. Glory to GOD for he answers Prayers!!

Don't give up!   Chapter 9

I remember a time while in the Navy. A year had gone by, and I felt that things were going smooth for me. I finished boot camp, and I graduated from my A school. I was a Paralegal. I just knew I was in the right place in my life. I was sent to my first duty station. Camp Cali in San Diego. One of my first day of work I was so excited to be a part of something. I never felt as thou I ever fit in. As a child I always felt like I should be with nerds or different kids. Little did I know God was setting me up to be a part of the "Peculiar People". As my supervisor Chief Randall walked across the Hanger, we were greeted by a CWO (Chief Warrant Officer) Brown. He oversaw our squadron. CWO Brown was from Alabama. He was a true Alabamian with his southern drawl. I was shown my office. I arrived at my office at 21 and thought I had arrived. I did secretary work, file, answer phones, type letters etc. After about a week I was bored. I thought I had signed up to be a paralegal. I went to CWO and asked, Ok. I have my degree and I've finished the Naval Justice Program with honors so why am I not doing that job? His answer was "we don't need a Paralegal; we like things just the way they are." You can only imagine how I felt. He had crushed all hope I had. I walked the rest of the day in a daze. As I did that, I started to notice that people would do what they wanted as long as the higher up didn't know. They were good. I couldn't see myself as a part of that. My father once told me " Don't let anyone tell you NO." When I got home I kept hearing that. So I got home to look for another squadron that needed a paralegal. As days and months went by I was looking for another job. I was getting awards, At -a-girl, praise for my work I even got nominated for Petty Officer of the year. I kept praying. I kept being me. I had 6 sailors under me. They were all cool except one, 3rd Petty Officer

Jackson. She was built and she had a big butt and long hair. She had slept with the higher ups to move up in rank. It was sad but that is the way it was back then. They didn't care if they or you were married. It's not easy to call the kettle black. I too was initiated into the group. I thought he was different. Petty Officer Jackson came into my group the last day of acceptance. Her parents were tired of her running away. So, she was persuaded to join the military. At 17. She was shapely. She wore thick glasses and wore a long wig and pranced around like they own the place. She had to be brought down a few notches. One day I had a meeting in my office. Everyone was chatting as I brought the meeting to order. I passed out the daily information and gave everyone their duties for the day. No one seemed to be listening. I looked out the window and starred at the street it was beautiful August day. All a sudden I felt a since of relief. Out loud I said, " I don't have to do this"! It went silent from all the chatter of the personnel.. I said it again. I don't have to do this! I got up and escorted everyone out of my office. In rush fashion. I shut the blinds and started to pray. I knew he would answer! God let me know that I had completed my mission. It was time to move on. I saw the captain the next day. Captain Rogers and PO Jackson. Outta nowhere Captain Rogers says, "I hear you want outta here?

I stayed still in my chair and said just as calmly then stood at attention and said, Yes SIR I DO! Oh, you should have seen their faces as though they both had seen a GHOST! I am sure they did because I never leave home without him! (Holy Ghost) The whaling ghost had been praying and crying for years to leave, but.....GOD had other plans for me. Needless to say, GOD had made a way for me. I was Certain of it.   After the Captain sent me to Headquarters I remained calm and unbothered by anything or anyone. The Headquarters went so far as having a ultimatum or scare tack tick. 2*Colon, A Master Chief and a 1st Petty Officer in a room the size of a closet. Everyone had a seat. I was told I was square peg trying to fit into a round hole. Then he pulled a vanilla envelope out and laid it on the table. He told me I had 2 choices: 1 To quit and get my benefits and health insurance and all the perks I was due. 2 I could get fired and lose all my benefits and he would make it hard for me to work. While pushing the envelope toward me. The choice was obvious! But before I did, I wanted to know, "How can you say I'm a Fuck up? Why did I get nominated for "Sailor of the Year?" Just let me know. (In my ear I heard "GOD's got this) Funny I never got an answer and my answer was "oh and I'LL TAKE #1 Please." I QUIT! Asked to be excused and walked out! 1st Petty Officer Zares followed me to my desk then escorted me out the main door. As I walked the hall I was smiling and relaxed. Zares asked me, and free! "Why are you smiling? You just got Fired and Quit?? I said, "you just don't know who is relieved and relaxed and free. I knew that GOD had once again made a way for me. I did my job, and no one could tell me otherwise, GOD has a way of letting you know, "He's not finished with me yet!!!!

Like the word says 'NOT IN YOUR TIME BUT GOD'S TIME'

GOD didn't give up on me that day!

He's taught me not to give up on me ever!

Chapter 9

How do you know that it's really Love?

I was getting indoctrinated with my new company. When he walked into the room our eyes met yet I looked away and blushed, Trying to listen away and blushed. Trying to listen to my new boss. This man had a smile that wouldn't stop. "Nothing like a man with beautiful teeth. I said hello and he and the officer greeted me. It was lunch time. So officer Davis asked me out to lunch, I sweetly declined. I walked away with a smile. He watched me walk away. A week went by. I got settled in my new position. While I was walking to my office and there he was standing in my office with flowers. I asked How can I help you, Officer Davis? I just stopped by to welcome you to the new company and assure you could come to lunch or dinner with me, and we can hang out. Again, I said No. #2. As I bit my lip as he walked away.... I thought he's cute even had a bottom that wouldn't quit. It had been a while. So, I decided to make him earn it. Just lunch would never do. Seems as though every week Officer Davis would make an appearance. (Lol to personally pick up the mail for the admiral. I played along. We would have light conversations. After a couple of weeks, he asked me out to dinner. Well, I was on a budget. I brown bagged it every day that is why I never went to lunch with him. I told him I could cook. His eyes lit up. So, I went home and prepared the best dinner I could. Meatloaf, scallop potatoes, green beans. I made my one bedroom comfortable. So, I lit candles and everything was set. Officer Davis showed up a few minutes late. I was worried at first. But he showed up with style flowers and a bottle of white zinfandel. Dinner was awesome afterwards we talked and went across the street to the Atlantic ocean. Everything was perfect.

Before I knew it, he moved me out of my one-bedroom into a 2
which we shared with another couple. We never talked about our
relationship at work for fear we would be torn apart. Then one
Christmas our first he asked me to marry him. He was truly a
dream come true. It's funny but we are set up in every aspect of
our life. How do you ask?

   By our Faith! Of course! I love this man more than I
loved myself. More than Life and yes God. I gave my everything
to Lamonte. He could do me no wrong in my eyes. Trust they
were darker than rose colored glasses. I forgot about "Me". I let
this man control me. My mom <u>used</u> to say I was naive. There was
nothing that he could say that I didn't believe. I trusted him with
my life. Sat to say the feeling was never mutual. Things got
rough when time came up for me to go to sea duty. I came to
work to find out I was going to the USS Vulcan in Fla. Which
made the news as a dike ship. I was a married woman to a man.
No ship duty for me. So, I called D.C. recruiters and asked if I
could get overseas duty in Europe, Germany or Spain? Spain was
it. I would never take No for an answer. I've lived by this value
my whole life.

Remember I told you Lamonte controlled me. Well, he had
no power to stop my destiny or GOD! GOD taught me who and
who's I was. Those 2 years in Spain were the calmest I had had in
a long time. GOD fed me when I was hungry, clothed me, kept a
roof over my head but most of all he loved me unconditionally.
Life doesn't get any better than that. Back home Lamonte was
dealing with his demons. Life was tough for him. Even while
over there I begged him to come over to Spain with me. What he
had and wanted was more important than me. This is when I
realized that while I was in Spain. I found purpose and a peace

that I never had when I was with Lamonte. I had not found the Love of my Life in a man but in GOD and myself.

When you truly are in Love it should always be GOD + ME in that order.

Chapter 10

Some people are seasonal, some people change against the season....

Some people you think you know oh so well. Then they decided to turn left. All along you thought you were doing the right thing by going along with them. People I thought would never leave me, did. I walked around with a whole lot of time on my hands. I can't blame those seasonal people. I can be! Rest assured that they completed their mission. Now that I'm alone we talk so much more. I'm talking about my Lord! Jesus! My Alpha and Omega.

I questioned GOD why he took those people away from me? I now know that those people are brought in and out of my life for a reason. I need to learn or relearn something. Sometimes I'd rather not know. Listening to GOD when all the noise is silent by GOD, is where I feel safe. I was one of those who changed against the season. Always trying to be nice and give people the benefit of the doubt. Hard nowadays. People are questioning my decisions on what's best for me!!!!

But when God is speaking to you clearly with no distraction.... I can't help but to know he is with me.

Even during the time, I lived in Virginia Beach. This was a time where I lived the "Life of Riley!" I had a great job, my own place, car, life was a woot! I had a roommate, and she was a Jersey Girl frfr. Her name was Nicole. She was older than me and was one of those seasonal people. Sometimes she treated me like I was a teenager in my own home. My mouth would not dare talk back to her. I learned a long time ago that you treat people the way you want to be treated. "But did you know, it happens. If you are disrespectful to elders the same will happen to you. When you get to be their age. Nicole and I had a close relationship we were like mother and daughter in my mind. We used to go out to lunch, go to the Casino and party together. No, we were not gay, lesbian, bi or whatever else is out there. We just clicked. Living with here was cool for the first year. Around the middle of July. We had rent due, cars, utilities, insurance. We were always on time until then. As I went to the bank to pay bills. I did my half and noticed that Nicole half was not there. She got paid before me and would always have enough for herself. So, I didn't get it??? Nicole told me she would talk to me later that night. I said, cool. I got home early. Usually 6:30 pm Nicole made it in by 7pm. But that night was different. 7:30 I said, ok maybe she made a stop then 8pm maybe an accident? No devil I don't believe it! God said she was ok. Give her some spare time. Nicole had a large gambling problem. I don't know what or how she was making the rent and taking care of herself.

It was not my problem as long as she did. I always seem to be the person to help. At this time, I was struggling myself so I could only do my half. So, there I was not feeling alone for the first time. You see GOD was with me and there is no way to explain it! All I know is if you just be patient and let him guide you with everything, he has for you!

You've got to know that everyone has their own story. But as long as you tell the truth and can be honest with yourself (stay humble) everything will be alright!

I had to remind myself that I had been here before and BUT GOD! Nicole had the problem, not me. I did what I could, and I didn't ask for something she couldn't give. Life has been clear to me. Especially when she told me that she was moving. All I said was "OK". That is your decision. So, I learned that Nicole came into my life as a seasonal person. You really don't know a person until you live with them. Learning this was a hard pill to swallow. I thought people like family would be the ones that hurt you. Talk about purging. Now is the time when people and things are taking over your mind and life.

Some people like my friend Terri. She was a beautiful person inside and out. She was a quiet, somewhat shy person. No one would dare say anything bad about her. This was only because we never saw her unless there was a basketball game. She would be a wallflower until the team came out. Terri was tall and had long red hair that was always in a ponytail. She wore the latest fashions. She had a car and a job. Terri would always live like, "she owned it."

Chapter 11

What I now Know………

I'm at a stage of my life where I hear him more clearly. My heart says Yes, but my mind is telling me "Wait a minute". And so, I pray. I have distractions.   I told you before "GOD has a way of telling you snippets of what is going to happen next part of my journey is going to be like. I can only speak for myself. Funny that's how I got here! My assignments are what I call them. Yes, you have to do the work!

So, if my family ever says "I'm like a gypsy, then tell them I was!

A gypsy for Jesus! I'm proud of every decision that was made by and for me! Because it was made just for ME! Because you really don't know what kind of GOD I serve until you try him for yourself!

Chapter 12

Enough is Enough

I finally learned what I heard years ago. I finally learned what I heard. Let me explain. You must hear before you learn anything!

1. I learned how to Love me 1st.
    - The things I've been thru.

2. I learned how to trust GOD!
    - Hearing his words!

3. I learned not to be regrettable.
    - Because everything I've done was a lesson learned for someone else or me or both.

So, both this I leave for my CHILDREN AND GRANDCHILDREN

"Put GOD 1st in everything you do....   Everything!"

"Never ever stop dreaming!!!!!!

"When you feel Enough is Enough and you want to quit. Just know there is so much for you."